C000173369

RASPBI

BEGINNER'S GUIDE

A Comprehensive Guide for Beginner's to Master
the New Raspberry and Set Up Innovative Projects

ALEXIS
RODRÍGUEZ

CONTENTS

INTRODUCTION i

CHAPTER ONE 1

About Raspberry Pi 4 and 3 1

    What is Raspberry Pi? 4

    Your new desktop computer 7

CHAPTER TWO 9

Raspberry pi specifications... 9

    Software and OS 13

    Compliance 14

CHAPTER THREE...16

Features of Raspberry Pi 4 and 3 16

    New RAM, CPU 18

    New GPU Faster Graphics Performance...................21

CHAPTER FOUR 23

Capabilities of the Raspberry Pi 4 and 3 23

    How is Raspberry Pi 4 and 3 different from others?.26

    Using Raspberry Pi 4 and 3 as a desktop PC 31

    Working on Raspberry Pi 4 and 3.............................34

CHAPTER FIVE.. 37

Browsing the web with Raspberry Pi 4 and 3 37

Using Raspberry Pi 4 and 3 as a media center 39

Running Raspberry Pi 4 and 3 on PS1, NES, SNES, N64, and console games 42

Operating system to run on Raspberry Pi................ 43

Raspberry Pi 4 and 3 on Windows 10 44

Raspberry Pi 4 and 3 running on windows 10 desktop apps 46

CHAPTER SIX.. 49

Raspberry runs on Ubuntu.. 49

Getting the most from your Raspberry Pi 4 and 3 ...50

Getting help with the Raspberry Pi 4 and 3 52

Keeping the Raspberry Pi 4 and 3 up to date........... 53

CHAPTER SEVEN 55

Raspberry kits availability 55

Power consumption of the Raspberry Pi 4 and 3 56

Power supply on Raspberry Pi 4 and 3 57

Fastest Micro SD card for Raspberry Pi 4 and 3 58

Size of Micro SD card for your Raspberry Pi 4 and 3 59

CHAPTER EIGHT... 61

Wi-Fi on Raspberry Pi 4 and 3 61

Running a network on Raspberry Pi 4 and 3 63

Are Raspberry Pi4 and Pi 3 64-bit?..........................64

CHAPTER NINE 66

Who is the Creator Raspberry Pi?...............................66

Raspberry Pi, just a motherboard? 68

Knowing the version of Raspberry Pi you have 68

Using Raspberry Pi 4 and 3 to learn to program.......69

CHAPTER TEN...70

Program hardware on Raspberry Pi.............................70

Raspberry Pi 4 and 3 for speech recognition............71

Building a cluster of Raspberry Pi 4 and 3 boards 73

Training a neural network with the Raspberry Pi 4 and 3 75

Running a neural network and learn machine on Raspberry Pi 4 and 3 76

CHAPTER ELEVEN 78

Where to purchase the Raspberry Pi 78

Availability of Raspberry Pi 5 79

Backward compatibility...79

Game emulation 80

CHAPTER TWELVE 82

Major differences between Raspberry Pi 4 and 3 82

Raspberry Pi design 83

Storage performance.............................. 87

Network performance 90

Power and heat 92

GPIO pins.. 95

Web surfing.. 95

Web hosting 96

Compiling code...................................... 97

CHAPTER THIRTEEN 98

10 things to know about Raspberry Pi 3...................... 98

Overlocking the Raspberry Pi 4 and 3................... 106

Raspberry Pi RAM you need................................. 107

CHAPTER FOURTEEN 109

Why Raspberry Pi 4 and 3 are important 109

CONCLUSION... 112

ABOUT THE AUTHOR 114

INTRODUCTION

Pi is several small single-board computers that were manufactured in the United Kingdom by the Foundation of Pi. The Raspberry Pi possesses a lot of features that can serve you well.

The Raspberry Pi has a lot of operating systems, which include the likes of NetBSD, Linux, FreeBSD, OpenBSD, Plan 9, and RISC OS. It also has a micro SDHC slot that provides for storage.

The Raspberry Pi that was manufactured by the organization has two arms. The CEO of the Raspberry Pi Foundation, Eben Upton, developed the Raspberry Pi to teach students in schools computer science.

In this ebook, you will get updated and informed about how both the Raspberry Pi 4 and Pi 3 run and work.

CHAPTER ONE

About Raspberry Pi 4 and 3

Let us begin with the Raspberry Pi 4. The Raspberry Pi 4 is the newest version of the Raspberry Pi. The Raspberry Pi 4 is very affordable as it has a low cost attached to it. It is certainly not your typical form of device, and it is cheap enough for you to buy.

Also, the Raspberry Pi 4 does not have a case, and it is known as a credit-card-sized electronic board, the kind you may see inside a laptop or PC, but always small in size.

The Raspberry Pi 4 cost is as low as $35. However, you might decide to purchase the $55 cost version because it possesses 4GB of RAM, which provides for the best performance.

For the Raspberry Pi 3, it is more of a development board that comes with the Pi models. The Raspberry Pi can be seen as a single-board computer that works on the Linux operating system.

The Pi 3 board does not only have a lot of features attached to it, but it also has an amazing processing speed, which makes applications efficient. The Pi 3 board is majorly produced for engineers and hobbyists who have interests in the system of Linux and the internet of things.

What is Raspberry Pi?

The Raspberry Pi, as you all should know, is a credit-card-sized computer produced and designed by the Raspberry Pi Foundation. The Raspberry Pi Foundation is not profit inclined, and it has the job of manufacturing computers and programming instructions to a large number of people.

The initial aim of the Raspberry Pi project was to manufacture computers that are not costly with its programming capabilities in student's hands. However, in recent times, the Raspberry Pi has been taken by the society at large.

The first of its kind was manufactured in 2012 has a system on a chip set up, which was built in the area of Broadcom BCM2835 processor, which is a small, powerful mobile processor popularly used in smartphones.

Raspberry Pi 3 image

It has the feature of a GPU, CPU, audio/video procession, and a low power chip, which is paired with a 700 MHz single-core ARM processor. The Raspberry Pi is an all-round device that has more hardware into a less costly body, and it is perfect for DIY projects.

Your new desktop computer

The performance and pace of the Raspberry Pi 4 is a whole new development from other versions like the Raspberry Pi 3. The Raspberry Pi 4, unlike other versions, has full experience for desktop.

The new Raspberry Pi 4 is silent through its fanless characteristics, and it is also energy efficient. You can run silently with the new Raspberry Pi 4, and it also makes use of lower power than other models of raspberry.

While purchasing the Raspberry Pi 4, you can decide the amount of RAM you require you to enable you to run your computer smoothly. You can either select a 1GB, 2GB, or 4GB RAM for your usage.

CHAPTER TWO

Raspberry pi specifications

Raspberry Pi 1GB, 2GB, and 4GB RAM

The Raspberry Pi 4 comes with a lot of specifications which are outlined below:

- OpenGL ES 3.0 graphics
- Operating temperature: 0 – 50 degrees C ambient
- Power over Ethernet (PoE) enables (needs different PoE HAT)
- 5V DC via USB-C connector (least 3A)
- 5V DC via GPIO header (least 3A)
- 2-lane MIPI CSI camera port
- 2-lane MIPI CSI display port
- micro-HDMI ports (supporting up to 4kp60)
- 2 USB 3.0 ports; 2 USB 2.0 ports

The Raspberry Pi 3 specifications are listed below:

- CPU: 1.2GHz quad-core 64-bit ARM Cortex A53
- Chipset: Broadcom BCM 2837
- USB: Four USB 2.0 with 480Mbps data transfer
- Ethernet: 10/100 (Maximum of 100Mbps)
- Display Interface (DSI)
- Video: Full HDMI port
- Camera Interface (CSI)
- Expandability: 40 general-purpose input and output pins

- Audio: Addition of composite video and 3.5mm audio out jack
- Memory: 1GB LPDDR2-900 SDRAM
- Storage: MicroSD card or through USB attached storage
- Wireless: 802.11n Wireless LAN (Peak transmit/receive all through 150Mbps) and Bluetooth 4.1
- Graphics: 400MHz Video Core IV multimedia

Software and OS

Those sets of users who are new to the Raspberry Pi 4 should begin with the NOOBS installation manager. The NOOBS makes it possible for the user to have a whole lot of options of operating system to select from the standard distributions.

The SD card with the new out of box software pre-installed can be purchased from any global distributors, or you can also choose to download it.

The recommended and advisable operating system you should make use of on a Raspberry Pi is the Raspbian. You can get assistance to download and install the Raspbian on your Pi.

Also, you can check out some instances on the internet to assist you in getting started with a few of the software which can be obtained in Raspbian. Get to know more about the Raspbian operating system when you read about the Linux usage and commands for moving about the Raspberry Pi and also managing the system of files and users alike.

Compliance

A lot of extensive compliance testing has been gone through by the Raspberry Pi 4, and it has succeeded in meeting several international and regional standards.

CHAPTER THREE

Features of Raspberry Pi 4 and 3

Raspberry Pi 4 showing HDMI port

The major new features of the Raspberry Pi 4 are the GPU and the faster processor, faster and much more RAM, extra USB 3 ports, double micro HDMI ports rather than a single HDMI port connection, and also support for 4K output.

The much-increased speed that enables the USB 3 support also permits the onboard Ethernet port to support Gigabit connections, which is also 125 Mbps while the older models have just 41 Mbps. Also, the micro SD card slot is two times as fast, which gives you a maximum of 50 Mbps as compared to 25 Mbps.

The new Raspberry Pi 4 charges over USB Type C rather than the micro USB. The Pi 4 also needs a power adapter which can give a least three amps of power as well as 5 volts. However, you can also make use of 2.5 amps if you do not attach a lot of peripherals to the USB ports. The USB Type-C can be reversed, which provides for it to be easy for children and grownups to plug in their USB cables.

New RAM, CPU

The latest model of the Raspberry Pi (pi 4) has related dimensions and designs to its former models; however, it is a new platform from others. The Raspberry Pi 4 is powered by the latest processor identified as the Broadcom BCM2711B0. The first

Raspberry Pi was released I 2012, and ever since, all versions of the Raspberry Pi has made use of 40nm Socs. The Raspberry Pi 4 differs as it possesses a new chip of 28nm process and not the former Cortex-A53 microarchitecture, makes use of Cortex-A72.

Raspberry Pi 4 has BCM2711B0, which has four cores while clocked at 1.5 GHz, and it is relatively faster than the Pi 3, which has 1.4 GHz BCM2837B0.

The new Pi, which has Cortex A72, possesses 15 instruction pipeline depth as concerning 8 on the older version, and it also gives out of order. This means that it does not wait for the result of other output before it begins another order.

Take, for instance, the Linpack benchmark, which has a measurement that totals power. The Pi 4 beats Pi 3 in the entire test conducted. The single-precision test recorded that Pi 4 has 925, compared to Pi 3, which has 224, and so it had a difference of 413.

When a Sysbench CPU test was carried out, it was discovered that the Raspberry Pi 4 could perform the function of 394 events per second while the Pi 3 can only perform 263 events per second.

The difference in RAM of the Raspberry Pi 4 and Pi 3 is quite large. Pi 4 also has higher bandwidth and more memory for surfing the internet. Raspberry Pi 4 RAM reads and writes 4130 and 4427 Mbps.

New GPU Faster Graphics Performance

The latest GPU is also very good. Formally, it runs on a Broadcom Video Core IV, which was effective on a clock speed of 400 MHz, but now runs on Video Core VI that has a clock speed of 500 MHz.

The new GPU permits it to output to a display at close to 4K resolution, which has a rate of 60 fps or to support two monitors close to 4K 30 Hz.

The Raspberry Pi 4 has a 720p, which makes it easy for the delivery of a smooth frame rate.

CHAPTER FOUR

Capabilities of the Raspberry Pi 4 and 3

Let us start with what the Raspberry Pi 4 is capable of performing. A lot of things can be done with the Raspberry Pi 4. New tech enthusiasts make use of the Pi boards as file servers, retro games consoles, media centers as well as network-level ad-blockers for beginners. Meanwhile, that is just a tip of the iceberg of what you can do with the Raspberry Pi 4.

As all know it, the Raspberry Pi 4 is a whole lot faster than other models of Raspberry, and this makes decoding 4K videos easier. Also, it benefits from much faster storage through the USB 3.0 and much quicker network connections through Gigabit Ethernet. Users may opt to make use of this. The Raspberry Pi 4 is the first of its kind that is capable of supporting 2 screens at once. It is also capable of having up to two 4K @30 displays for uses that need and requires a little more space on your desktop.

Now to turn attention, we now focus on what the Raspberry Pi 3 is capable of performing. The Raspberry Pi 3 is capable of performing the function of a media center, budget desktop, router for beginners, and retro games console. Just like you have it in the Raspberry Pi 4, there are a whole lot of projects which the Pi can do. For example, the Raspberry Pi 3 can build robots, phones, tablets, and laptops. The Raspberry Pi 3 and 4 are very similar in what they are capable of doing or performing. However, they still possess some level of differences, which are not all that noticeable with just a glance.

How is Raspberry Pi 4 and 3 different from others?

The quad-core Raspberry Pi 4 is very much capable and faster than other models of the Raspberry. Unlike other models of the Raspberry Pi, the Raspberry Pi 4 has a new board and can play a 4K video at 60 frame every second while boosting the Pi's center media.

Meanwhile, that is certainly not an assurance that all 4K videos played will be very smooth for viewing. The Raspberry Pi 4 supports hardware acceleration (speed) for H.265-encoded video is presently going on well in all the Pi's series of operating systems, which makes it an enticing feature in the models to come than what the Raspberry Pi 4 already has.

The Raspberry Pi 4 has a new board, unlike other models of the Raspberry Pi, which can boot directly from a USB-attached pen drive or hard drive. Besides, after a future firmware update, the Raspberry Pi 4 will be able to support booting while making use of PXE. Making good use of a network-attached drive is perfect for remotely updating your Raspberry Pi 4 and also to share OS images between two machines alike.

Let us dive into question on how the Raspberry Pi 3 is different from other models like the Raspberry Pi 2. The Raspberry Pi 3 has a much faster quad-core, and it is much more capable and efficient that the models before it like the Raspberry Pi 2.

Users who have an interest in benchmarks, the Raspberry Pi 3 CPU, which is the major board processor has about 50-60 % much-improved performance in 32-bit mode, than other models such as the Pi 2. Also, the Raspberry Pi 3 is 10x faster than the initial single-core Raspberry Pi, which is a multi-threaded CPU benchmark in SysBench.

Compared to the first models of the Raspberry Pi, the real-world applications will have a much better and higher performance of about 2.5x for one threaded application and higher than 20x when the video playback is much faster by the chip's NEON engine.

Unlike other former models of the Raspberry Pi, the Raspberry Pi 3 has a board that is capable of playing 1080p MP4 video at 60 frames every second (having a bitrate of around 5400Kbps), while boosting the Pi 3 media center credentials. The performance of the playback of the video is dependent on the source video, as well as the player that was used and the bitrate.

Just like the Raspberry Pi 4, Pi 3 also supports wireless internet out of the box because of its built-in Wi-Fi and Bluetooth, which is embedded in it. The Raspberry Pi 3 can even boot directly from a USB attached pen and hard drive. Lastly, the Raspberry Pi 3 supports booting from a network-attached file system making use of PXE, which is important and necessary for having to remotely update your Pi and also to share an operating system image among different machines.

Using Raspberry Pi 4 and 3 as a desktop PC

The Raspberry Pi 4 can perform the function of running as budgeting of desktop, and the latest model, which is Pi 4, has made it very efficient.

The Raspberry Pi 4 as a desktop pc is the biggest advantage of using every day in web browsing, office applications, and online access service.

Since the Raspberry Pi 4 has the feature of a 4GB RAM, it does no longer have issues with heavy web pages and applications. It is also capable of switching between full online services without having to buff. It is different to using a PC as it is much expensive than the PC. The Pi 4 has a much-improved specification than the former models.

The Raspberry Pi 3 can also be run as a budget desktop if you have the patience to wait. Meanwhile, since the Raspberry Pi 3 is not the latest model of the Raspberry Pi, do not have high expectations that the Raspberry Pi 3 will work on the same level as the PC.

It is ever likely to lag while loading heavy websites and whenever you want to browse some sites that have a lot of workloads. If you run more than one tab at a time, you run the risk of overloading the memory of your Pi, which will make it lag and freeze for a long period.

Working on Raspberry Pi 4 and 3

It is possible to work on your Raspberry Pi 4. The slow movement from software to online services, the web highly the only application that a computer requires to run, and on the front of the Raspberry Pi 4.

Some weeks following the release of the Raspberry Pi 4, the places which are not on the Raspbian desktop tend to have a relation to the video playback. Meanwhile, it will be sorted out by a future software update.

Also, the Raspberry Pi 4 works as a thin client as it has been run with its capabilities when it is running as a thin client for Windows 10 with the performance closely different from running a new Windows 10 PC, save for gradual transfer of the data to USB. The Pi 4 model has a Gigabit Ethernet and will certainly work well as a thin client.

You can also work on a Raspberry Pi 3; however, it is a matter of time before it will begin to wear because when you start to load web pages and moving from one tab to another and applications will not be going as fast as expected.

Even while you can run all the applications you wanted open, you still focus on web applications, and people who make use of applications cannot see the supported Pi Linux-based OS. Also, the Raspberry Pi 3 works well as a thin client, just like the Pi 4. It was confirmed after successful testing of the thin client for Windows 10.

CHAPTER FIVE

Browsing the web with
Raspberry Pi 4 and 3

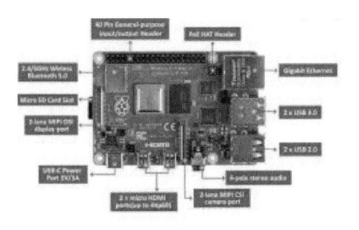

Properly labeled Pi 4

You can browse the web with the Raspberry Pi 4 because it has the new and up to date official OS version, which has the Chromium browser as well as the browser that the Chrome uses. Like was stated earlier, the Raspberry Pi 4 has excellent performance and minor lagging on heavy sites, with the only problem being the YouTube video launching, but it will be corrected in the next update.

With the Raspberry Pi 4, you can also browse with the older model of the Pi 3. The Raspberry Pi 3 official OS is powered on as it has the Chromium browser. The performance is quite useful if you do not open a lot of websites so that it does not begin to lag. The Pi 3 also has extensions that permit for a smooth-running playback of video on YouTube as well as other websites.

Using Raspberry Pi 4 and 3 as a media center

There are more than enough options if you wish to make use of the Raspberry Pi 4 as a media center. However, the most common and used options include Kodi based Oses OSMC.

Also, the Raspberry Pi 4 has more advantages and positives of a much faster and up to date CPU and graphics processor in which the Foundation of Raspberry Pi has stated that the Pi 4 is capable of playing local H.265-encoded video recorded at 3840 x 2160 resolution and also 60 frames every second.

Meanwhile, the support for the above acceleration is not fully entrenched in all the Pi's operating systems, and it is a gradual process. More advantages of the Raspberry Pi as a media center are because of its built-in support for Wi-Fi. The support for Wi-Fi makes it very simple and stress-free to stream content to the Raspberry Pi 4 and the native

Bluetooth males hooking up to the peripherals much easier.

Just like the Raspberry Pi 4, the Raspberry Pi 3 also has different options if you wish to make use of the Pi 3 as a media center, and the most used and famous option is the LibreElec or the Kodi based Oses OSMC.

Also, the Raspberry Pi 3 has more advantages as it possesses a slightly faster graphics processor that can play local H.264 encoded video, which can be recorded at 1920 x 1080 resolution and 60 frames every second. Recall that the Raspberry Pi 4 plays a local video at H.265-encoded video recorded at 3840 x 2160, which makes it more advanced than the Raspberry Pi 3.

Meanwhile, the Raspberry Pi 3 also has easier streaming content because of it's built-in support for Wi-Fi.

Running Raspberry Pi 4 and 3 on PS1, NES, SNES, N64, and console games

The Raspberry Pi 4 and Pi 3 can run on PS1, NES, SNES, N64, and other console games with the assistance of emulators such as RetroPie with also few games from the systems outlined. However, if the system is new, it has every chance more demanding things will be difficult.

Operating system to run on Raspberry Pi

Both the Raspberry Pi 4 and Pi 3 can run on a lot of systems, which include the official Raspbian OS, Snappy Ubuntu Core, LibreElec, and the Kodi based media centers OSMC, Ubuntu Mate and the non-Linux based Risc OS. Also, the Raspberry Pi 4 can run the Windows 10 IoT Core.

Raspberry Pi 4 and 3 on

Windows 10

Windows 10 can run on the Raspberry Pi 4 and Pi 3. However, be warned that it does not possess the full desktop version of Windows 10, which the majority of people use and know. The Raspberry Pi 3 model, which is the former model before the Pi 4, runs Windows 10 IoT Core, which is a lower version of the Windows 10 that does not boot into the graphical desktop; it is made and produced to be controlled through a command-line interface on a remote computer.

The Pi 4 and Pi 3 models can run only on a single full-screen Universal

Windows Platform application one by one and not simultaneously. Take, for instance, a kiosk application for a retail store; however, other kinds of software can be run but in the background.

The Raspberry Pi 4 and Pi 3 can also act as a Windows 10 thin client. It is possible as the Windows 10 can run on a server and streamed to the Pi 4 as well as with a secure server. What you are likely to go through in this process will be very similar to running a Windows 10 machine. Since the Raspberry Pi 4 and Pi 3 has more power and also its dual display support, the co-producer of Raspberry, Eben Upton, made it clear that he expects to undergo research into the thin client market.

Eben Upton, the co-producer of Raspberry Pi, stated that he thinks the Pi 4 and Pi 3 has the power to be able to run a full desktop version of Windows on Arm. However, he also said that the choice to port Windows to the Raspberry Pi 4 depends solely on Microsoft.

Raspberry Pi 4 and 3 running on windows 10 desktop apps

Yes, the Raspberry Pi 4 and Pi 3 can run on Windows 10 desktop applications. However, the Pi 4 and Pi

3 version can only run on Windows 10 desktop apps if enough effort is put into it. Also, the apps are likely not to run well because of the effort that has to be put in.

Formally, the Raspberry Pi 4 and Pi 3 can be possible to do so while making use of the ExaGear Desktop software, but it can no longer be found in the market. Pi386, among other options, are free to be used.

There are a lot of ways you can make use of, but the performance of running Pi 4 and Pi 3 on windows 10 desktop apps is sub-par. Note that the tools which you will require to run Windows 10 desktop apps on Pi 4 and

Pi 3 will need a lot of processing power, which you are not given a chance to. It is likely to be possible, but it is not advisable to be done.

CHAPTER SIX

Raspberry runs on Ubuntu

The Raspberry Pi 4 can run Ubuntu with different desktops. The Foundation that runs the Raspberry Pi stated that Ubuntu Snappy Core and Ubuntu Mate as the basics.

Getting the most from your Raspberry Pi 4 and 3

You have to take care of your Raspberry Pi 4 and Pi 3 to prevent it from damages, especially if you will be transporting it from one location to another. Be aware that the Raspberry Pi 4 does not fit the previous models of the Raspberry Pi cases because there was a change in the layout.

If you have a knack about an excellent performance for your Raspberry Pi 4 and Pi 3, you should go in search for a high-speed micro SD card,

The Raspberry Pi 4 and Pi 3, as you should know by now, can run as many operating systems as possible. For users of the Pi 4 and Pi 3 who are after a good performance, stability, and quicker system, the official Raspbian operating system is the best option for you. The introduction of a fast web browser and efficient programming software are also some of the things you can get from your Raspberry Pi 4 and Pi 3.

For those Raspberry Pi 4 and Pi 3 users who did not install the Raspbian OS while making use of the NOOBS installer and you lack space, you can opt to visit the terminal and type 'sudo raspi-config' and move ahead to choose the option in order to 'Expand root partition to fill SD card'. After that is done, you will then begin to use the open space on the SD card.

Getting help with the Raspberry Pi 4 and 3

The first Raspberry Pi model was sold in 2012, and since then, there are over 27 million boards which have been sold. The Raspberry Pi board now brags a potent society that assists its users through the official Raspberry Pi website and forums alike. If you are seeking to get help with the Raspberry Pi 4 and Pi 3, you should visit the official Raspberry Pi website and forums for information and assistance.

Keeping the Raspberry Pi 4 and 3 up to date

As a Raspberry Pi 4 and Pi 3 user and you are running the Raspberry Pi official Raspbian operating system, keeping your Raspberry Pi 4 or Pi3 is relatively easy, and you should not worry too much about it. What you are required to do as a Pi 4 and Pi 3 user is to open the terminal and type sudo apt-get update. Whenever the update is completed after typing the outline command in the terminal, go ahead and also type sudo apt-get dist-upgrade to keep up to date.

CHAPTER SEVEN

Raspberry kits availability

You cannot lack the Raspberry Pi kits because they are readily available. It has a lot of things ranging from robotic arms, virtual assistants, speech recognition, $35 board, and also build-it-yourself laptops for children. Based on the success of the Raspberry Pi, if you have any idea for a project, there should be a kit that will fit your needs and requirements.

Power consumption of the Raspberry Pi 4 and 3

With a view of tests that have been conducted and completed, the highest power consumption of the Raspberry Pi 4 is around 7.6W under load and also 3.4W when it is not in use.

For the Raspberry Pi 3, after the conduct of tests, it is known that the highest power consumption of the Raspberry Pi 3 when it under a lot of loads is around two times that of the former model (Raspberry Pi 2) which is 750mA VS 360mA. Meanwhile, when there is a lower workload, it is almost the same as the former boards.

Power supply on Raspberry Pi 4 and 3

The most sought after and best option for power supply on Raspberry Pi 4 is the official Raspberry Pi Foundation USB Type-C power supply. It is, however, rated at 5.1V/3A.

While the best option for power supply on Raspberry Pi 3 is the official Raspberry Pi Foundation power supply. It is, however, rated at 2.5A5.1V. Meanwhile, the previous boards were rated at 2A5V.

Fastest Micro SD card for Raspberry Pi 4 and 3

There is a much quicker micro SD card for Raspberry Pi 4. The major fast micro SD in new research for Raspberry Pi 4 is known to be the 32GB Samsung Evo+. However, it is very cheap, and it is known to be less than $10.

To the fastest micro SC card for Raspberry Pi 3, there is a major micro SD card in new research, which is known to be the SanDisk Extreme PLUS 64GB microSDXC. You should also take note that the SanDisk Extreme PLUS 64GB microSDXC is expensive than others micro SD as it goes for $58.95, which is way much expensive than the actual price of Raspberry Pi 3.

The majority of users of Raspberry Pi 3 make use of a standard class 4 micro SD card, which works around 4MB/s can go a long way.

Size of Micro SD card for your

Raspberry Pi 4 and 3

For the Raspberry Pi 4 and Pi 3, the size of the micro SD card you should get if you seek to install the official Raspbian OS is nothing less than an 8GB micro SD card. Meanwhile, users who seek to use the Raspbian Lite, a minimum of 4GB should be the size of micro SD to be used.

CHAPTER EIGHT

Wi-Fi on Raspberry Pi 4 and 3

Fully labeled Raspberry Pi 3

Yes, users of the Raspberry Pi 4 can make use of Wi-Fi. Wi-Fi can be run on Raspberry Pi 4 as the board supports about 802.11ac Wireless LAN (around the region of 100 Mbps) as well as Bluetooth of 5.0.

For users of the Raspberry Pi 3, Wi-Fi can also run on it as the board supports a different Wireless and Bluetooth connection. For the first, it supports 802.11n Wireless LAN (maximum of about 150 Mbps) as well as Bluetooth of 4.1.

Running a network on Raspberry Pi 4 and 3

It is possible to run a network of Raspberry Pi 4 and Pi 3. Also, updating and managing the boards is much easier to be able to boot from a network-attached file system while making use of OXE, permitting administrators to be able to share and distribute operating system pictures between the machines.

There will be the addition of a PXE support in a firmware update in the later years to the Raspberry Pi 4.

Are Raspberry Pi4 and Pi 3 64-bit?

This is one of the most frequently asked questions by users of the Raspberry Pi. The Raspberry Pi 4 and Pi 3 are 64-bit. Meanwhile, there are some limited advantages to the 64-bit processor, not around a little more operating system that are likely to run on Raspberry Pi 4 and Pi 3.

Instead of putting and giving out a 64-bit model of the official Raspbian operating system, the Foundation of Raspberry Pi has stated that they want to fix their attention on optimizing the Pi's official Raspbian OS for 32-bit performance to become advantageous to thousands and millions of former versions. Meanwhile, the 32-bit Pi boards are already in the market and are selling.

CHAPTER NINE

Who is the Creator Raspberry Pi?

The Raspberry Pi boards are produced by a part of the Raspberry Pi Foundation, which is known as a charitable organization giving their all to increase the level of computer science education. The Raspberry Pi is manufactured and produced at a Sony factory located in South Wales. A lot of schools have adopted the Raspberry Pi since it was launched, and it is readily available for use. The production of Raspberry Pi has made more than enough number of people to apply to Cambridge University to study computer science.

The pioneer of the Raspberry Pi Foundation, as well as the co-founder Eben Upton, stated that he started designing the board because he wanted to inspire kids to learn about computing because he was not happy with the low applicants in Cambridge to study computer science around 2000.

Raspberry Pi, just a motherboard?

The Raspberry Pi is a motherboard, and you can get it for $35 as other motherboards you can get around. However, there are various kits of Raspberry Pi in which you can purchase. Meanwhile, the official Raspberry Pi 4 starter kit goes for 90 Dollars, which possesses a case, bar the monitor, mouse, and keyboard.

Knowing the version of Raspberry Pi you have

You can easily see the version of the model of Raspberry Pi you have because it is written on the top side of the upper edge of the board, below the 40-pin header.

Using Raspberry Pi 4 and 3 to learn to program

We should be aware that the Raspberry Pi official Raspbian OS is embedded with software that is capable of tutoring its users on programming, which includes the drag and drop coding tool scratch as well a different utility for debugging and writing while making use of Python programming language.

CHAPTER TEN

Program hardware on Raspberry Pi

It is possible to program hardware on Raspberry Pi via the row of 40 GPIO, which means General Purpose Input Output pins situated at the top edge of the board. Hardware, which includes sensors, motors, and LEDs, can be joined to the pins for the interaction to take place with the Pi. Writing easy programs will permit you to either send or receive signals while making use of the pins. For instance, to produce an LED flash or to also go through measurement from an attached sensor.

Raspberry Pi 4 and 3 for speech recognition

The Raspberry Pi 4 and Pi 3 are very much capable of performing speech recognition. A popular open-source option known as 'Jasper' can be chosen to be installed on the Pi and be opened and made use of without having to connect to the internet.

The majority of options for speech recognition have their hope on a cloud service, meaning that it needs an internet connection to perform its operation. Examples may include Alexa Voice Service or Google Speech.

One of the simplest ways to add speech recognition to the Pi is through Google's Voice AIY, which means the Artificial Intelligence Yourself kit. The Google Voice Artificial Intelligence Yourself kit gives all the additional hardware which you require to change the Raspberry Pi into a Google voice assistant.

Building a cluster of Raspberry Pi 4 and 3 boards

It is possible to build a cluster of Raspberry Pi 4 and Pi 3 boards. You can save more money when you join eight (8) boards together into an Octa Pi cluster. Note that when power has been combined, it makes for a much faster cluster board than just one (1) board when you calculate prime factors, a major task when you seek to crack encryption code.

The long end of the scale is 750 Pi clusters, which have been produced at the Los Alamos National Laboratory, and it will soon raise high to about 10,000 boards in a few years to come.

If you do not know how to build a cluster of Raspberry Pi 4 and Pi 3, there is a guide for you on how you can develop and make your own Octa Pi.

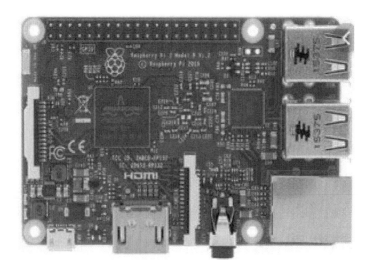

Training a neural network with the Raspberry Pi 4 and 3

The Raspberry Pi 4 and Pi 3 is not strong enough to teach neural networks or to perform any useful operation. It is more advisable to make use of a faster and powerful computer that has a mid to high-end graphics processing unit (GPU) or also a cloud computing instance which includes AWS P3 or also a Google Cloud Platform Cloud and Tensor Processing Unit.

Running a neural network and learn machine on Raspberry Pi 4 and 3

It is possible to run a neural network and also learn machine on the Raspberry Pi 4 and not the Pi 3. Meanwhile, as a Pi 4 user, you should invest in a few additional hardware for it to be effective and productive. For instance, Google's Coral USB stick, which fastens the rate in which Pi operates situations that has to do with vision, which includes object and facial recognition while making use of its specialized cores. It is capable of fastening machine learning models produced while making use

of Google's Tensor Flow Lite library.

CHAPTER ELEVEN

Where to purchase the Raspberry Pi

You can purchase the Pi 4 model for $35 - $55 as it is available through its official resellers. As a potential user of Raspberry Pi, you can check out the guide when you purchase the Raspberry Pi. Also, the Raspberry Pi 3 sells for 27 to 30 Euros through the RS Components and Premier Farnell.

Availability of Raspberry Pi 5

The Raspberry Pi 5 is not yet available, and it will not be available for some years to come because of the time of other older models. The latest model of Raspberry Pi you can find in the market for purchase is the Raspberry Pi 4.

Backward compatibility

It is vital to be aware that even some months after the launch of the Pi 4, there are still a few basic Raspberry Pi 4 software that does not always work. For you to be able to make use of the Raspberry Pi 4, you will be required to download a new production of the Raspbian OS, Raspbian Buster.

Meanwhile, it is not all of the things that run in the Raspbian Buster yet. While tests were conducted, the discovery of a lot of Python libraries or some needed packages that were not compatible with the latest Raspbian OS.

Game emulation

There is a very common gaming emulator software known as Retropie. Note that Retropie, the gaming emulator software, is not in support of the Pi. A research was conducted, and it was discovered that you could run Retropie on Pi 4, but it is presently known that it does not work as previously stated.

A beta model of the Lakka can be downloaded but on a different emulation platform, and it is not known to be working effectively. People who develop the Raspberry Pi have stated that they are looking to make a Pi 4 compatible version, and they will develop one in a short time from now.

CHAPTER TWELVE

Major differences between Raspberry Pi 4 and 3

Chapter thirteen talks about the major differences between Raspberry Pi 4 and Pi 3. Here, we will take a look at the differences in the CPU, GPU, USB ports, and so on.

CPU: The Raspberry Pi 4 runs on 1.5GHz

CPU: The Raspberry Pi 3 runs on 1.4 GHz

Video Out: Raspberry Pi 4 has dual micro HDMI ports

Video Out: Raspberry Pi 3 has a single HDMI port

Power requirement: Raspberry Pi 4 has 3A and 5V

Power requirement: Raspberry Pi 3 has 2.5A and 5V

Raspberry Pi design

As outlined earlier, the Raspberry Pi 4 size is 3.5 x 2.3 x 0.76 inches (88 x 58 x 19.5 mm) and also 0.1 pounds (46 grams), which makes it possible for it to enter your pocket and it is also light in weight to be carried to all places.

The Raspberry Pi 4 board is durable to make it stay in your bad; however, you should stick it in a thing which can protect and guide it, especially to safeguard the pins. Meanwhile, while testing the board and Pi 4, the board bare is always on the table, and it is moved front and back between my place of work and office alike as it places it in a cardboard box that has no static or padding bag.

Sadly, if you require a case, you cannot make use of the board that has been designed for older Raspberry Pi. The Raspberry Pi 3 and 4 + are known to have similar dimensions; however, the port layout differs just so that the latter can be incompatible.

The older models of the Raspberry Pi have a single, full-size HDMI port, the double micro HDMI connectors found on the Raspberry Pi 4 do not interfere with the Pi 3 model. There is a case that costs $10 and 8.50 in Euros, and it is known as Pimoroni Pibow. It is known to be very good, but the fault with it is that it does not cover the GPIO pins.

The Raspberry Pi 4 is known to cover a lot when the ports come into question. The Raspberry Pi 4 right-hand side has four USB Type-A connections, two of the four USB

Type-A connections are USB 3.0. Also, there is a full-size Gigabit Ethernet port that serves as a wired connection. The lower edge of the Raspberry Pi 4 has a 3.5 mm audio jack, USB Type C charging port as well as two micro HDMI ports. On the left-hand side of the Raspberry Pi 4 is a micro SD card reader.

On the top surface of the Raspberry Pi board is, you will be able to view the ribbon connectors for the Camera Serial Interface (CSI) as well as a Display Serial Interface (DSI) which provides for connections to Raspberry Pi's screen and camera and compatible accessories.

Furthermore, it is possible to connect a camera to a USB port, and there are some popular methods of making it possible such as the micro HDMI ports and output to a screen.

Storage performance

It does not matter how the rate at which your processor, GPU, and RAM run if you possess slow storage, you will find it very difficult if you want to open your applications and files alike.

All Raspberry Pi, the micro SD card reader, is the Pi 4 storage device, which makes for its convenience but somewhat restricted.

The Raspberry Pi Foundation made it clear that Pi 4 has a high transfer rate of 50 Mbps, which is two times the speed of the card reader on Pi 3. There is no certain limit on the capacity of Pi 4.

Some experiments were done with a Samsung EVO Plus micro SD XC class 10 card, which displayed fewer rates than the maximum. The Pi 4 read and write the rates, which includes 45.7 and 27.7 Mbps, respectively. The Pi 3 was left behind to read and write 22.8 and 17.5 Mbps respectively.

Users that have an external SSD or a fast USB flash drive, you will experience a much better storage performance on your Raspberry Pi 4. The Pi 4 has a whopping 3 USB ports which have a high bandwidth of 625 Mbps.

While making use of a Western Digital Blue SSD in a USB to M.2 enclosure, it was seen that the speed of transfer was recorded as 2 to 13 x faster than the original micro SD card. Also, the applications which were slow in responding and opening began to open much quicker with the SSD that was attached. Sadly, a normal USB flash drive is slower than the micro SD card.

You should be aware that currently, the Raspberry Pi 4 firmware does not permit one to boot off an external drive. The solution you will have to take is run all of your programs, which includes most of the OS.

However, note that there would be a firmware update in the coming months that will fix this issue. Quick USB 3 ports are much more and serve the function than just storage. The likes of Google's Coral USB Accelerator, which assists in artificial intelligence tasks, can be used.

Network performance

The new model of the Raspberry Pi has a similar 802.11ac Wi-Fi as its former model (Pi 3). However, it has

Bluetooth 5.0, which is more improved than its predecessor.

Also, the Ethernet port has much more bandwidth, which permits it to give out a full gigabit. When the Ethernet port of the Raspberry Pi 4 was tested, it arrived at 943 Mbps, which is much more greater than other models of Raspberry Pi. Extensive research done showed that the Pi 4 achieved 943 Mbps while its closest competitor arrived at just 237 Mbps.

Since Raspberry Pi 4 and Pi 3 has the same 802.11ac Wi-Fi, which can run on 2.4 GHz bands, there is not much difference in performance.

Audio phones plugged to Pi 3

Power and heat

The Pi 4 model is known to consume more power than the former models because it has a more power-hungry processor. When the Raspberry Pi 4 is idle, it collects about 3.4 watts, which is about 17% more than the former Pi

3. Meanwhile, when the Raspberry Pi 4 is under load and active, it rises to 7.6 watts. Meanwhile, it is still a little 19% better than the Pi 3.

Users of Pi that need a lower power Pi, the Pi Zero W, is the best for you as it consumes only a small 0.8 watts when it is idle and 1.66 when it is active and under load.

The board in Pi 4 is much warmer than the former models. The areas of the Pi 4 board close to the CPU is often warm, not only the top of the processor that gets warm. The Raspberry Pi 4 has up to 74.5 degrees Celsius, which is not enough for it to heat up and possibly burn. While Pi 3 has up to 62.5 degrees Celsius, which is lower than the new model.

A CPU intensive workload was tested for 10 minutes, and it was seen that the processor got to 81 degrees and started to go down from 1.5 to 1 GHz after a couple of minutes. Meanwhile, the processor began to regain itself to 1.5 GHz when it came down to 80 degrees.

When the Pi is active, it is advisable to get an active cooler for your Raspberry Pi, or you can attach a passive heat sink.

GPIO pins

The new model pins support four extra 12C, SPI as well as UART connections. You can get a much quicker response and speed with the GPIO pins on the Raspberry Pi 4 because of its faster processor.

Web surfing

The web surfing you get on the Pi 4 is much better than you will get with other models because of its faster processor. The Pi 4 runs on 4GB RAM as compared with other older models, which makes surfing the web faster and enjoyable.

Web hosting

It is not difficult to set up a Raspberry Pi web server, and it is one of the most common cases of a computer. You can get the best when it comes to web surfing because of its fast processor and better RAM capacity.

You can open heavy pages and serve guests simultaneously because it gives 3983 requests per second than 2850 that the Raspberry Pi 3 gives. A lot of web apps make use of the PHP server-side scripting language. That means a much faster and quicker processor can assist the PHP in some way. You can get the best of hosting web pages on your Pi 4 and other older models.

Compiling code

Having Linux, in some cases, you will have to compile programs you wish to install. A lot of instances, when testing is done, there is a need to compile software packages so that an object recognition demo can start.

For the Raspberry Pi 4 to compile code quicker, a faster processor and much better RAM is needed, and it is efficient in Pi 4 than other older versions.

CHAPTER THIRTEEN

10 things to know about
Raspberry Pi 3

Pi 4 full case

Chapter fourteen begins with the
Raspberry Pi 3 as you will get to know

ten things about the Raspberry Pi 3. They include:

1. The Raspberry Pi 3 is a mini-computer which was designed by the Foundation of Raspberry Pi. The Raspberry Pi Foundation is a charitable organization situated in the United Kingdom. With just a token, you will get the best out of the computer as it possesses mind-blowing features such as the processor RAM and graphical capabilities.

2. With the Raspberry Pi 3, you can almost perform every operation. The Raspberry Pi is for global use, and you can get the best from it.

3. Another thing to know about the Raspberry Pi 3 is that its storage is sold differently. There is onboard storage, which is not available with the Raspberry Pi. The former Pi models made use of a full-sized SD cards, but the latest versions, including the Pi 3 made use of a micro SD card.

4. The Raspberry Pi 3 requires accessories. As you need your personal micro SD card, you cannot connect the board to anything at all. The likes of things you will need include: Display and Connecting cable, Keyboard, mouse, monitor, Micro SD card, Power supply, Pi case, and Ethernet cable.

5. One major thing you should know about the Raspberry Pi 3 is that it makes full use of a 5.1 V micro USB power supply. However, the 5V might be better than the 5.1V. Any

good 2.5 Amp power supply is good enough and will be effective enough. The Pi 3 makes use of more power supply than its former models.

More Amps can be eaten up if the Pi 3 runs on a heavier load and if you add more USB.

6. Users of the Raspberry Pi 3 do not need to know Linux. If you are not sure of a certain thing, the Raspberry Pi has a website that can serve as an assistance to you in helping you to get started.

Meanwhile, if you make use of the vanilla Raspbian OS, the majority of the pre-built OS has all tools which can be found in the image. The kind of information you will be required to supply is Wi-Fi connection information.

7. Raspberry Pi 3 has improved connectivity, power management, and performance. The Pi 3 model costs almost the same as the Pi 2 model, but they are relatively different. For example, the Raspberry Pi 3 is 50% faster than the Pi 2

model, but both the Pi 3 and the Pi 2 have 1 GB of RAM as well as a fourth-generation Video Core GPU. However, the quad-core, which the Pi 2 possesses 900 MHz CPU, was upgraded to 1.2 GHz CPU.

8. Pi 3 has GPIO plug-in expansion board, which makes for extra functions, which includes sensors, sound or video cards, power relays, and so many others. Other peripherals such as touch screens, GPS antennas, retro

USB NES controller, and cameras can also be found.

9. The Raspberry Pi 3 has a dedicated monitor that is not needed. As a user of Pi 3, and you go to set up, you have to plug your mouse and keyboard into the USB ports on the Pi 3 and go-ahead to connect it to a monitor through an HDMI. Typically, it will lead to the booting of some operating systems as well as other graphical user interfaces (GUI). It is not all the project that you need the Raspberry Pi, and you can

make use of the GUI and permit you to operate it in headless mode.

10.   In Pi 3, you will have to look out for the pin. If you are calling pins from the line of command, be aware that Pin 1 found on your Pin out header does not equal to PIO.

Overlocking the Raspberry Pi 4 and 3

The major thing to know when you are overlocking both the Raspberry Pi 4 and Pi 3 is that you can easily achieve the 1.5 GHz CPU, increasing it to 2 GHz and get the frequency to be higher from 500 to 600 MHz. Endeavor that you possess a fan such as the Pimoroni Fan Shim.

Raspberry Pi RAM you need

You can get the Raspberry Pi 4 in three configurations, which are closely related to the amount of RAM. You can get the $35 price model for 1GB RAM, while the $45 has 2GB of RAM, and the last unit of $55 goes for 4GB of RAM.

One of the best reasons to use the Raspberry Pi is because of its less cost as well as its efficiency. If you are going on light surfing of the web, the 2GB RAM is the best option for you.

However, the 4GB RAM is the best for a user of the Raspberry Pi who is looking to embark on a more difficult task, which may include A.I.

CHAPTER FOURTEEN

Why Raspberry Pi 4 and 3 are important

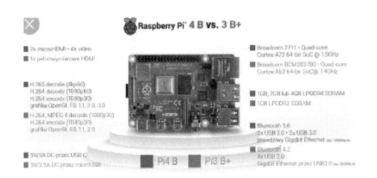

Comparison between Pi 4 and Pi 3

There are a lot of reasons why both the Raspberry Pi 4 and Pi 3 are essential. Mere taking a look at the features and the specifications, you will see reasons to make use of either the Raspberry Pi 4 or the Raspberry Pi 3. Whichever one you choose, it is very efficient and less costly than what you will get for their other kinds out there.

The Raspberry Pi 4 and Pi 3 are important for users because it seeks to give you the best in what you are in search of. The RAM and fast web surfing should be more than enough reason as to why both Pi 4 and Pi 3 are important. Other features and specifications are, however, also stated to fit your desire and cover your taste.

CONCLUSION

You can get the best out of either your Pi 4 or your Pi 3. Certainly, Pi 4 has a whole lot of benefits which surpasses the Pi 3, but, that does not make the latter less important and effective than the former (Pi4).

Choose the model that fits your style and enjoy it because both of the models are fantastic and amazing in their way. I see no reason why the Raspberry Pi 4 and Pi 3 should not be in your mind today. Take out your money and purchase the less costly Pi 4 or Pi 3 depending on what your budget can cover, and you will not regret it.

ABOUT THE AUTHOR

Alexis Rodriguez belongs to a group of Tech editorial team and is already testing the echo loudspeaker before its market launch.

Gathering experience with innovati-ve Ambient Assisted Living devices while studying and blogging about it for many years.

In addition, in 2017 he wrote the first comprehensive overview of Alexa compatible devices. Vacuum robots, smart home cameras and remote-controlled garden tools are also among his favorite subjects today.

Printed in Poland
by Amazon Fulfillment
Poland Sp. z o.o., Wrocław